Scary Creatures
BEARS

Written by
Dr. Gerald Legg

Illustrated by
Mark Bergin

W
FRANKLIN WATTS
A Division of Scholastic Inc.

NEW YORK • TORONTO • LONDON • AUCKLAND • SYDNEY
MEXICO CITY • NEW DELHI • HONG KONG
DANBURY, CONNECTICUT

Created and designed
by David Salariya

CL

Author:

Dr. Gerald Legg holds a doctorate in zoology from Manchester University. He worked in West Africa for several years as a lecturer and rainforest researcher. His current position is biologist at the Booth Museum of Natural History in Brighton, England.

Artist:

Mark Bergin was born in Hastings, England, in 1961. He studied at Eastbourne College of Art and has illustrated many children's non-fiction books. He lives in Bexhill-on-Sea, England, with his wife and three children.

Series Creator:

David Salariya was born in Dundee, Scotland. In 1989, he established The Salariya Book Company. He has illustrated a wide range of books and has created many new series for publishers in the U.K. and overseas. He lives in Brighton, England, with his wife, illustrator Shirley Willis, and their son.

Cover Artist:

Carolyn Scrace

Editors:

Stephanie Cole
Karen Barker Smith

Photo Credits:

B & C Alexander, NHPA: 11
Bill Coster, NHPA: 21
John Foxx Images: 24
Martin Harvey, NHPA: 29
T Kitchin & V Hurst, NHPA: 8
Gerald Lacz, NHPA: 14
Andy Rouse, NHPA: 12, 17, 18, 22, 25, 28
Kevin Schafer, NHPA: 10
John Shaw, NHPA: 9, 13, 15

Created, designed, and produced by
The Salariya Book Company Ltd
Book House
25 Marlborough Place,
Brighton BN1 1UB

Visit the Salariya Book Company at
www.salariya.com

A CIP catalog record for this title is available from the Library of Congress.

ISBN 0-531-14667-7 (Lib. Bdg.)
ISBN 0-531-14847-5 (Pbk.)

Published in the United States by Franklin Watts
A Division of Scholastic Inc.
90 Sherman Turnpike
Danbury, CT 06816

Printed in Italy.

Printed on paper from sustainable forests.

Contents

What Is a Bear?

Bears are mammals. They are related to dogs and wolves. Most bears are large animals with big heads, round ears, and small, forward-facing eyes. Their large bodies are supported by short, strong legs. Bears also have powerful claws.

X-Ray Vision

Hold the next page up to the light and see what's inside a polar bear.

See what's inside

Mammals are **warm-blooded** and keep their body at a high, constant temperature. They have fur, or hair, that keeps them warm. Bears are warm-blooded and covered in fur. That means they are mammals.

Is a bear a mammal?

Yes, a bear is a mammal.

Is a bird a mammal?

No, a bird is not a mammal.

Birds are also warm-blooded, but they have feathers instead of fur.

4

powerful jaws

big paws

claws

thick fur

strong legs

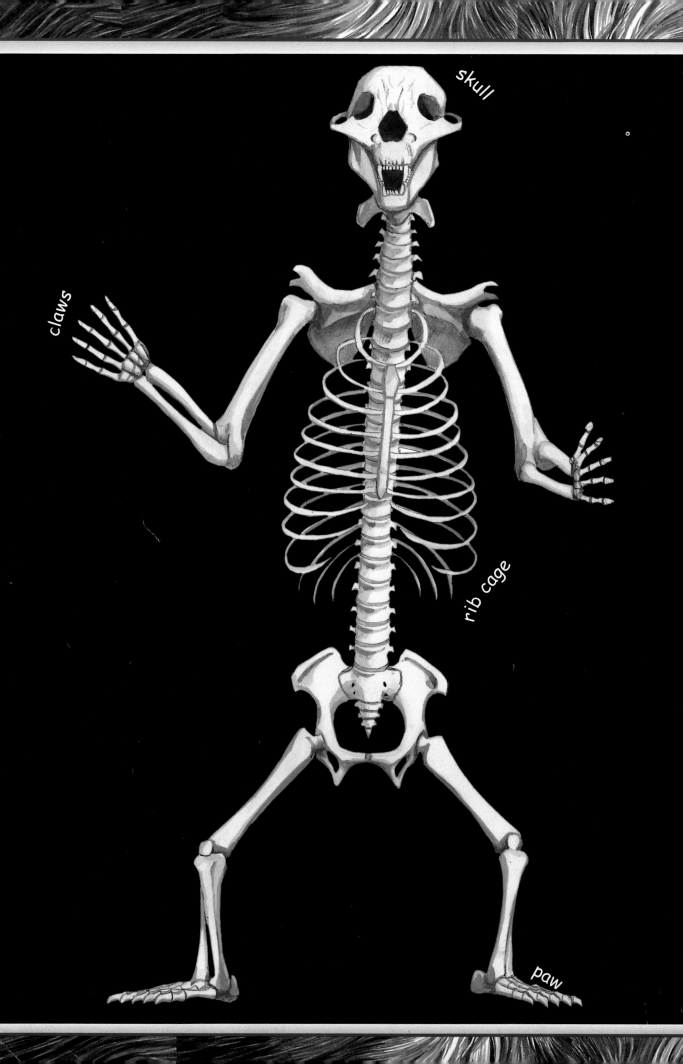

What's Inside a Bear?

Bears, like all mammals, have a bony skeleton. The head and skull are supported by the neck, which is part of the backbone. The backbone ends in a short tail.

A wide, strong rib cage protects the lungs, heart, liver, and other organs. Bears' paws are very big. They have five toes that end with sharp claws.

The skeleton of a bear allows it to stand upright, like people do.

Did You Know?

Our cuddly teddy bears are modeled after the brown bear. They are named after President Theodore Roosevelt, who refused to shoot a cub on a hunting trip in 1902.

A bear skull

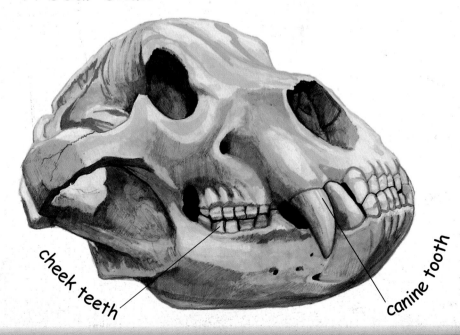

cheek teeth

canine tooth

Bears have very strong skulls (left). Huge jaw muscles are attached to the skull. These make the bear's head very big. Bears have sharp **canine teeth** and broad, flat **cheek teeth**. That is why bears can eat any type of food they like.

Why Are Bears Scary?

Bears are big, strong, clever, and bad-tempered. They can easily kill other animals and people with their powerful claws and teeth. If you accidentally get too close to a bear you might frighten it. This could cause it to attack without warning. Most bears are scared of people, so making plenty of noise will keep them away.

Did You Know?

If a bear sees you and lowers its head, this is a sign that it is about to attack. Don't crouch down or the bear will think you are about to attack too!

Which bear is the scariest?

American brown bears, including grizzly bears, are among the largest living land **carnivores**. They can weigh up to 1,874 pounds (850 kg) and stand over 9 feet (2.8 m) tall, making them very scary. They will not hesitate to attack. Polar bears are the most aggressive bears of all. They are not afraid of anything!

Brown bears and polar bears are the scariest!

A fierce brown bear growling

This large brown bear opens its mouth and growls a warning to other bears. He is protecting his territory and letting other bears know that he is in charge.

What Do Bears Eat?

Bears will eat just about anything, including small mammals, insects, **carrion**, fruit, grass, roots, leaves, and even people's garbage.

A bear uses its front paws as eating tools. Their sharp claws can catch and hold **prey**, tear trees open to look for insects, dig for roots and **grubs**, rip flesh, and even catch fish.

Giant panda eating bamboo

Did You Know?
Sun bears are very noisy eaters. They make a noise so loud that it can be heard several miles away.

Giant pandas (left) spend 10 to 12 hours a day eating about 31 pounds (14 kg) of their favorite food, bamboo. They can eat up to 40% of their body weight! Sometimes they eat other plants, and occasionally small mammals and fish.

Polar bears like to eat seals. They sniff out baby seals that hide in the snow and wait patiently for them to come out of their breathing holes in the ice.

In the summer, polar bears eat fish, birds, eggs, and some plants. They will also eat dead walruses and whales that they might find. Polar bears eat more meat than any other type of bear.

Polar bear eating an eider duck

Where Do Bears Live?

Polar bears live in the Arctic regions. Other bears can be found in the **tropical** forests of India, Sri Lanka, and Southeast Asia, or the mountains of South America. They also live in the **temperate** forests of Southeast Asia, Europe, and North America.

Did You Know?

In Britain, as in many parts of the world, bears have been hunted to **extinction**. They were last seen in Britain 1,200 years ago.

Polar bears (below) have to walk long distances across the Arctic ice in search of food. Food can be very hard to find in these surroundings.

Polar bear walking across the Arctic ice

Brown bears live in temperate forests, but they can also live in other areas such as the open plains, **tundra**, and **subalpine** mountain areas of North America, Europe, Japan, and North Asia. They used to live throughout Europe and North America, but there are fewer of them now because of hunting and the destruction of their **habitats**.

brown bear in the mountains of North America

Are Bears Good Hunters?

Most bears are very good hunters. The polar bear is the best. It is very patient and can sneak up on its prey quietly. Brown bears hunt small mammals and can even attack deer, moose, and young buffalo.

A brown bear showing its big teeth

Smaller bears also hunt small mammals, fish, birds, and insects.

Did You Know?

Brown bears living on the islands of Kodiak and Admiralty, Alaska, are the largest land carnivores in the world. They are up to a third larger than their mainland cousins.

Brown bears hunting for fish

How do bears catch fish?

Did You Know?

Grasshoppers, crickets, beetles, and caterpillars are favorite foods of the American black bear. These, finished off with some honey, acorns, blueberries, and mountain holly make a delicious meal.

Brown bears are excellent at fishing (above). When the salmon are swimming upstream they catch the fish with their paws, or snatch them with their mouths as the fish leap the **rapids**. The bears can catch and eat so many fish that they gain a lot of weight.

Bears catch fish with their teeth and their claws!

Is a Panda a Bear?

Yes, a panda is a bear. Until 1995, scientists thought that the giant panda was a member of the **raccoon** family rather than a bear.

The giant panda is almost dependant on one type of food, bamboo. To crush this tough plant, pandas have powerful jaw muscles and special, flattened cheek teeth. Bamboo naturally dies off every few years making it difficult for pandas to find food. This, along with habitat loss and **poaching**, has reduced their population to about one thousand.

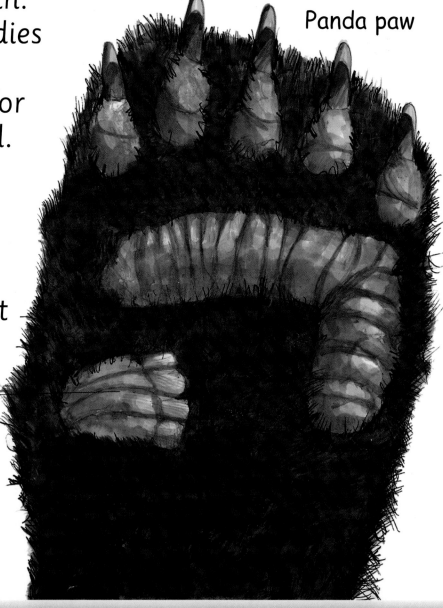

Panda paw

extra sixth toe

Pandas are unusual because they have six toes on their front paws. The extra toe lets them hold onto bamboo stalks.

Giant pandas in China

Did You Know?

When first born, a baby bear is tiny. A baby panda is the smallest of all the bear species, weighing only 3-5 ounces (80-140 g) at birth.

A panda's diet is almost entirely made up of bamboo shoots and bamboo roots. They also eat other plants including flower bulbs, grasses, and occasionally fish, insects, and small rodents.

Are Bears Good Parents?

Bear cubs are raised by their mothers. The mother bear will keep her tiny, newborn cubs warm with her long fur. She will also teach her cubs what to eat, how to find food, and how to catch prey.

X-Ray Vision

Hold the next page up to the light and see what's inside a pregnant bear.

See what's inside

Polar bear with cubs

Did You Know?

Mother bears are very protective of their cubs. Black bears send their cubs up a tree if there is danger. Sloth bears carry their cubs away from danger on their backs.

A pregnant brown bear

powerful shoulder muscle

ribs

lung

developing cubs

When Do Cubs Leave Their Parents?

Newborn cubs stay with their mother in their **den** until early spring. The larger bears such as the polar, black, and brown bears, nurse their cubs until they weigh about 4 pounds (2 kg).

Learning about their new world takes time, so most cubs stay with their mother for at least two years. After that they are on their own. They will start their own family four to seven years later.

Brown bear nursing her cubs

Sows, or female bears, usually nurse their cubs while laying on their back or on their side.

What Do Bears Do in Summer and in Winter?

In the summer, life is easy for most bears. They have a wide selection of food to eat such as leaves, flowers, fruit, and small animals. During the late summer and early fall, some bears start to prepare for their long winter sleep by eating a lot and storing up fat.

Did You Know?
The American black bear must add at least 4 inches (10 cm) of fat to its body before its long winter sleep.

Brown bear cubs are born in the winter. In the summer, they explore their new world with their mother and grow strong. It is a time to relax, explore, play, and eat.

Brown bear cubs playing

For many bears, winters are cold and food is hard to find. So they find a safe, sheltered cave or hollow tree to sleep through the winter in. Bears do not really **hibernate** because their body temperature and heart rate stay the same. The temperature of true hibernators falls close to that of their surroundings, and their heart rate slows down.

Female bears also spend time in the winter looking after and feeding their newborn cubs.

Did You Know?

A bear can sleep for several months in its den, living off the fat it gains during the summer. It may lose 15%–40% of its body weight just by sleeping.

When winter starts, the female polar bear digs her den in the snow and sleeps (right). In late November, or early December, she gives birth to twins. She is a good mother and she stays with the cubs for several weeks without eating.

A polar bear and her cubs in the den

Why Are Polar Bears White?

The polar bear's white fur is very important. It camouflages, or hides, the polar bear as it hunts its prey across the snow and ice or waits for animals to come out of their shelters.

The polar bear's white fur also protects a layer of warm, yellow wool. Furry soles protect the polar bear's feet against the cold and help them grip the ice.

Polar bear

Did You Know?

Although they look white, polar bears have black skin, and a black tongue and nose to trap heat. The white fur is actually **translucent** and lets the warming sunlight through to the black skin where it can be absorbed.

Do polar bears get cold?

Beneath the polar bear's skin there is a thick layer of fat. This, along with a warm coat of fur, keeps a polar bear warm even in the coldest weather. Temperatures can get as low as -40°F (-40°C).

No, polar bears never get cold.

Did You Know?

Despite their size, polar bears are very fast runners. They can outrun a reindeer over short distances and swim at 2.5 miles per hour (4 kph).

Polar bear in the snow

Bears Around the World

Polar bears are found in the Arctic regions.

Brown bears are found in more parts of the world than any other bear. They live throughout the cool northern forests of the United States, Europe, Japan, and North Asia.

Bears live all around the world from tropical forests to the icy Arctic.

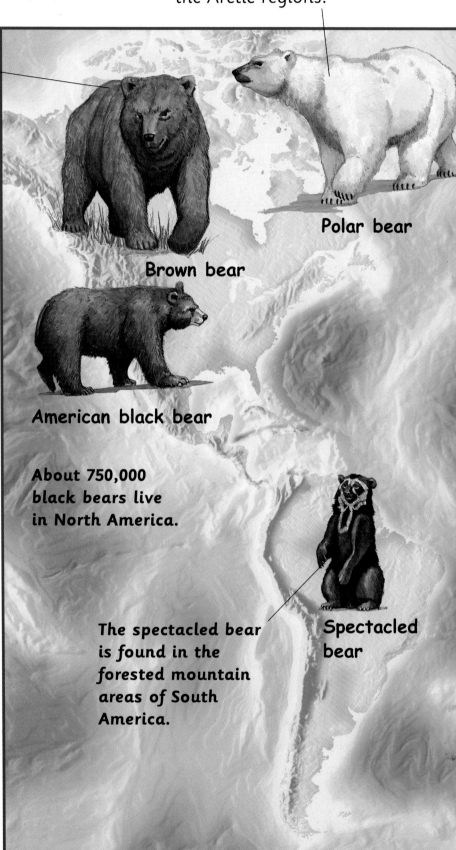

Brown bear

Polar bear

American black bear

About 750,000 black bears live in North America.

The spectacled bear is found in the forested mountain areas of South America.

Spectacled bear

Pandas are only found in small regions of southwest China. They live in an area that covers about 5,328 square miles (13,800 square km).

Brown bear

Asiatic black bear

Panda

Asiatic black bears are found throughout hilly, forested areas of Southern Asia.

Sloth bear

Sun bear

Sloth bears live in the the forests and grasslands of India and surrounding countries.

The sun bear is the smallest type of bear. It weighs about 220 pounds (100 kg). It is found in the tropical rainforests of Southeast Asia.

What Are Bears Scared Of?

Bears have very few enemies. Most bears die from accidents and diseases. However, thousands of bears are shot for "sport" in North America every year, making humans their worst enemy.

Many bears are kept in **captivity**, often in poor conditions, so they can be used to entertain people.

A sun bear caged in Taiwan

Bears are very intelligent animals and can be trained very easily when they are young. This often means that the mother is killed so that her cub can be kept.

Training is often cruel and bears hate to be kept in small spaces or cages.

Did You Know?

In Asia, bears are killed so that parts of them can be used in traditional medicines.

Did You Know?

Six of the eight species of bears are close to extinction. Even the other two species, the brown bear and American black bear, are currently threatened.

This Asiatic black bear is performing in New Delhi, India (right). In many parts of the world, it is illegal to use animals in this way.

A performing black bear

Bear Facts

Brown bears can tear open a locked freezer to get the food inside.

Brown bears have an extremely good sense of smell. The part of the nose that is used to pick up scent is 100 times bigger in a bear than in a person.

Black bears are not always black. They can be brown, white, and even blue!

Spectacled bears build themselves platforms out of branches in the treetops. They use these platforms as places to feed and sleep.

Sun bears have no hair on the palms of their paws. This makes it easier for them to hold on to the trees they climb.

People often think that the koala is a bear. The koala is, in fact, closely related to the kangaroo and is not a bear at all.

The sloth bear's diet is almost entirely made up of termites. It can shape its **muzzle** into a tube and use it to suck termites from their nest.

The polar bear's front paws are webbed like ducks' feet. This makes them very good swimmers.

Polar bears have a second, clear eyelid. It protects their eyes while they are swimming, like built-in goggles.

Female bears are called sows and males are called boars.

Spectacled bears will climb cacti to taste the sweet fruit at the top.

 # Glossary

canine teeth The two pointed teeth on either side of the mouth located at the front of the jaw.

captivity When an animal is kept in a cage.

carnivore An animal that hunts and kills other animals for food.

carrion The rotting flesh of a dead animal.

cheek teeth The teeth in the back of the jaw used for crushing and chewing.

den A hollow tree or cave used as a place to sleep.

extinction When a species of plant or animal is no longer alive.

grubs A wormlike larva of some insects.

habitat An animal's natural surroundings.

hibernate When animals spend the winter months sleeping in a nest or shelter. An animal's breathing and heart rate slow down when it is hibernating.

muzzle The part of a bear's face that sticks out and forms the nose and jaw.

poaching Illegally hunting animals.

prey Animals hunted and killed by other animals, called predators, for food.

raccoon A badger-like carnivore that lives in North America.

rapids Fast flowing part of a river where the water rushes over rocks.

sow The name for a female bear.

subalpine The parts of mountains below the cold rocky area, but above where trees grow.

temperate An area of the world that has a warm or hot summer and a cool or cold winter.

translucent Almost see-through.

tropical An area of the world where it is usually hot all the year round.

tundra The cold area north of the Arctic circle where few plants grow.

warm-blooded An animal whose temperature remains almost the same, whatever the temperature around it.

Index